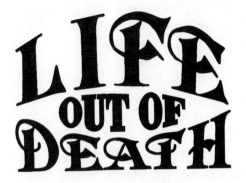

LIFE OUT OF DEATH

A brief summary of
Madame Guyon's
SPIRITUAL TORRENTS
and other papers on
the Spiritual Life

By

JESSIE PENN–LEWIS

CHRISTIAN • LITERATURE • CRUSADE
Fort Washington, Pennsylvania 19034

CHRISTIAN LITERATURE CRUSADE

U.S.A.
P.O. Box 1449, Fort Washington, PA 19034

BRITAIN
51 The Dean, Alresford, Hants. SO24 9BJ

NEW ZEALAND
P.O. Box 77, Ashurst

Originally published by

THE OVERCOMER LITERATURE TRUST
England

First American Edition
1991
This Printing 1995

ISBN 0–87508–950–X

Scripture Quotations from:
The *American Standard Version* of the Bible, 1901, Thomas Nelson & Sons, New York, unless otherwise indicated.
The *King James Version* of the Bible (*KJV*).
The Epistles of Paul (a translation and notes) by W. J. Conybeare, England (died 1857).

PRINTED IN COLOMBIA

CONTENTS

PREFACES TO EARLY EDITIONS
OF *LIFE OUT OF DEATH* 7

Synopsis of *Spiritual Torrents* 11

1. LIFE OUT OF DEATH 15
2. THE WALK OF FAITH 27
3. THE NEW LIFE IN GOD 41
4. CHARACTERISTICS OF A
   SOUL IN DIVINE UNION 57
5. FOUR PLANES OF THE SPIRITUAL LIFE 69
6. WHAT "DEATH" WITH CHRIST IS NOT! 83
7. THE APPROPRIATION OF TRUTH 91

PREFACE

PART OF PREFACE TO FIRST EDITION, 1896

I AM constrained to publish this brief Summary of *Spiritual Torrents* by Madame Guyon under the ever-deepening conviction that it is much needed by many of the children of God at the present time.

The book itself, *Spiritual Torrents,* is too analytical, too involved in expression, too overdrawn, too mystical for general circulation, yet the deeply taught writer had definitely learned to diagnose God's dealings in the deeper walk of faith as few modern writers can.

May I give one word of warning concerning this Summary: In consulting a medical work, it is not necessary that *all* the symptoms of a disease be manifested in order to indicate the remedy. So also in this spiritual diagnosis. A sentence here and there may indicate the present stage of one's experience; then let the reader put the booklet aside for a time, and not ponder over it so as to induce introspection.

PREFACE TO REVISED EDITION, 1900

In reissuing this brief Summary of *Spiritual Torrents* it will be seen that I have practically recast the whole, not combining the early stages of the "Way of Light" and the "Way of Faith," as in the first edition.

I have also added, as chapter four, a few summarized extracts on the characteristics of the soul in union with Christ, as described by Prof. T. C. Upham in his book *Divine Union in the Higher Forms of Religious Experience*, as well as three additional chapters for further clarification.

The whole of *Spiritual Torrents* is written about the subjective aspect of the Holy Spirit's working in the soul, and it may be well to point out that the writer deals very little with the earlier stages of the spiritual life. In reading this Summary it is therefore of vital importance to apprehend first, and fully, our faith-position in Christ.

In the purpose and sight of God we *have died with Christ* (Romans 6:2-3). By faith in the working of God ("faith *wrought in you* by God"—Colossions 2:12, *Conybeare*), we are made partakers of His resurrection. Through His precious blood, by "a freshly slain and yet a living way" (Hebrews 10:20, Rev. C. A. Fox), we may now enter boldly into the Holiest of All.

As the Spirit of God reveals more fully the life of one's selfhood, and as the sacrificial knife (Hebrews 4:12, so the thought is in the Greek) of the living Word of God pierces to the dividing of soul and spirit, we must turn to the finished work of our Redeemer and thankfully recognize our place *with Him* upon His cross. Thus shall the Spirit of life in Christ Jesus make us *free,* and we shall be joined to Another, even to Him who was raised from the dead, that we might bring forth fruit unto God.

Also, we may be in spirit anchored "within the veil" in union with Him who has entered as our Forerunner, even while experientally we are being bowed under the hand of God—for He may be bringing us low in order to lift us up and lead us on to a fuller knowledge of Himself, even into that secret place of the Most High where God is All!

J.P–L.

"We possess by first being deprived; death precedes life; destruction in the spiritual experience turns to renovation. Out of the sorrows and silence of inward crucifixion, and from no other source, must grow the jubilees of everlasting bliss."

—Upham's *Life of Madame Guyon.*

A SYNOPSIS OF
SPIRITUAL TORRENTS

1. Conversion, and the description of three classes of believers.

2. Fuller description of the first class of believers, compared to feeble and sluggish torrents: those who deal with the outer life—draw from outward sources—are dependent upon meditation, reasoning, efforts.

3. Believers of the second class—the "Way of Light"—walking in the light of God. The senses are much involved in this degree. These individuals are full of fire and love, they use the terms of "death," and they have died so far as their own works and efforts are concerned, but *not so as to appropriate or possess nothing.*

4. Believers of the third class—the "Way of Faith"—compared to torrents of headlong impetuosity. They rest in nothing until they reach their goal. After much seeking and struggling, Christ is revealed within. The

soul seems overwhelmed with joy unspeakable, and full of glory. At this early stage there is much of the *emotional* life, and manifestations of God, which cease at a higher degree.

5. The imperfections of the first degree of the true "Way of Faith." The progress of the divine life beyond this point occupies the remainder of the book.

6. The second degree of the "Way of Faith," describing the alternations in experience.

7. The third degree of the "Way of Faith," describing the stripping of spiritual riches, until the person is on all points wrecked upon God.

8. The stripping of the garments of the individual, i.e., its old experience.

9. The stripping of the individual's self-admiration, through the beauty gained by previous gifts of God.

10. The loss of everything that self-love could cling to.

11. The soul brought to nothingness, and described as being in the tomb.

12. The fourth degree: the torrent in the ocean. The individual united to Christ in God. The gradual manifestation of the di-

vine life, the soul being revivified by degrees.

13. Further characteristics of the life of union. The liberty of the soul, its facility in service, its "ordinary" exterior, its unconscious spontaneity of life.

14. The same theme. The immovability of the soul, "rooted and fixed in God." God all in all.

15. The deepening of the life in God; union preceding fusion, or oneness, with Christ in God. The capacity of the soul, and its continued increase.

16. Concluding remarks concerning the Unitive Way. The necessity of shunning self-reflection, and of abiding in the love of God.

Editor's note: The use of the word "soul" in this work is not ordinarily to be taken as referring specifically to a part of man's being (i.e., spirit, soul, body), but rather as referring to the whole person, the individual as a whole, in his relationship to God.

Note 2: "mg."="margin." This indicates a marginal, alternative translation.

CHAPTER 1

LIFE OUT OF DEATH

A brief summary of *Spiritual Torrents*

Three classes of believers. The description of the first class. The second class called the "Way of Light." The third class called the "Way of Faith."

AS SOON as the soul has turned to God and has been cleansed from its sins, it instinctively desires to be entirely united to Him. Out of God it can never find repose.

There are three classes of believers, that may be compared to rivers flowing toward God as their ocean: (1) Some moving toward Him sluggishly and feebly; (2) Some proceeding decidedly and rapidly; (3) Some advancing with headlong impetuosity.

BELIEVERS OF THE FIRST CLASS

These Christians advance slowly and feebly. They deal much with the outward life, and are very dependent on outside sources of help. They are like pumps that give water only when worked. They are available for service only in conjunction with others. They have great desire to be always doing. At one time they do wonders, at another they only crawl. They are easily discouraged, and are often scrupulous and fettered by their particular abilities. They are full of plans as to how to seek God and to continue in His presence, but all this is by their own efforts, *aided* by grace.[1]

How to help these individuals.

They should be encouraged to seek God with intensity, and taught to think less of gaining the mental knowledge of God (i.e., gaining information about Him), than the knowledge gained by love.[2]

---

[1] This describes the "up-and-down" experience and fitful self-effort of many true children of God.

[2] The heart-life should be cultivated by prayer and loving trust in God, more than the intellectual life by study (1 John 4:7–8). These souls need to know the Holy Spirit in full possession (John 16:13–14), for the love of God is shed abroad in our hearts by the Holy Ghost given unto us (Romans 5:5).

THE WAY OF LIGHT

BELIEVERS OF THE SECOND CLASS

These are like large rivers which move with decision and rapidity, yet they are dull and sluggish compared with the impetuous torrent described later on. Believers of the second class are drawn out of the first (the feeble rivers), whether gradually or suddenly, by God taking hold of them.[3]

These persons are so full of light and ardent love that they excite the admiration of others, for God seems to give them gift upon gift, graces, light, visions, revelations, ecstasies. Temptations are repelled with vigor; trials are borne with strength. Their hearts are enlarged, and they gladly make great sacrifices for God and others.

The dangers in the "Way of Light."

These individuals are often admired too much, and their minds may be thus diverted to themselves. They easily tend to rest in the gifts of God, instead of being drawn to run after God through His gifts.

The design of God in pouring out His

---

[3]The description that follows clearly indicates the filling of the Spirit, and most beautifully points out the change from feeble self-effort to ardent love service.

graces so profusely is to draw them to Himself, but they sometimes make a different use of His mercies. They may rest in His gifts, look at them, appropriate them to themselves, and thus give place to vanities, self-complacencies, self-esteem, and preference of themselves to others.

The characteristics at this stage.

These persons are beautiful as regards themselves, and greatly help others, yet they often exact too much from them and are exasperated by their inconsistencies. *They are not able to help weak believers according to the degree (stage of development) they find them in,* and consequently may divert them out of the right path.[4]

Christians who have thus been taken hold of by God possess so much (and that so decidedly from *Him*) that they do not believe there is anything greater. They have much more difficulty in entering the life of pure faith than do the feeble ones, for they are loaded with spiritual riches.

They are firm in their opinions, and because their grace is great they are the more assured concerning them. They are discreet

---

[4] That is, by expecting them to "see" or "accept" spiritual things which may be beyond their capacity at the time.

and prudent, and carefully guard themselves from taking any wrong step. They often enjoy "interior silence," a delightful peace, and communings with God which they can easily describe.

They use the terms of death, and they do truly "die," as far as their own efforts are concerned, to the world and to all exterior things, but they have *not died to all interior possessions, so as to possess nothing except as in God.*

They desire to be "nothing" and to have deep humility, but this is more in the sentiment and not in the real inward meaning of self-effacement, for this sentiment and partial knowledge sustains the soul in its own life (Luke 14:26).

Some people in the "Way of Light" do not enjoy these abundant gifts but have simply a deep-seated strength and a gentle, peaceable, pervading love. Such persons are skilled in covering their subtle faults from themselves and others—by making for them some good excuse.

These rich souls do not often reach God as their only center while in this world. They are too loaded with His gifts, and few have the courage, after possessing so much, to consent to (apparently) lose all. *Esteem of our own spiritual possessions is an obstacle harder to be overcome than the greatest sin.*

God never violates our liberty, and so He leaves these souls to take pleasure in their own sanctity.

How to help these souls.

They need the heavenly vision of a deeper life in God, far beyond all this. They need to know that God gives them so much in the way of gifts *because of their weakness* rather than because of their strength. They should be gently led from the sensible (i.e., conscious) life, to rely upon the Divine life;[5] from the "perceived" (visible), to the very certain "darkness" (i.e., apparent blindness) of pure faith. They should be encouraged to lay no stress upon all their many experiences, nor to look at their gifts and graces, lest they rest in them for even a moment, but to pass beyond *them* to the *Giver* (Philippians 3:10; 1 Corinthians 8:2).

THE WAY OF FAITH

(The History of the Torrents)

BELIEVERS OF THE THIRD CLASS

These Christians are like "torrents" which

---

[5]Simply 2 Corinthians 5:7; 2 Corinthians 4:18. In the maturity of the spiritual life what seems "darkness" to the consciousness becomes clear light to the eyes of faith. We look not at the things "not seen" by the physical eye, nor are they felt by sense. "We walk

have their source in God, and enjoy not a moment's rest until they are lost in Him. Nothing stays their progress, and they run with a rapidity which strikes fear into the boldest. They are drawn from among the feeble ones (the first class), or from the souls in the "Way of Light"[6] *when any of these have courage to part with their rich experiences* and to press on to know God.

THE FIRST DEGREE[7]

God commences His work in a soul by causing it to feel the estrangement from Himself. It is given a true grief for its sins and sees a rest in God afar off, the sight of which redoubles its restlessness and increases the desire to reach that place of rest.

It seeks at first in outside means what it will never find except within. The wound is in the heart. Unsatisfied, these persons be-

---

by *faith*, not by appearance" (*ASV*, mg.).

[6] By the feeble ones receiving the filling of the Spirit, and souls in the "Way of Light" becoming thirsty for deeper knowledge of the Living God.

[7] The history of the soul is here retold from the beginning of its conversion under the figure of "Torrents," and the remainder of the book describes the progress of the Torrent toward and into God as the ocean. The "first degree" seems to comprehend the initial turning to God, and the revelation of Christ within the heart by the Holy Spirit.

come more eager, and struggle with all in themselves that hinders, but the fight only increases their sense of helplessness.

In the mercy of God, help is sent them, and they are instructed to seek *within* what they have looked for *without*; at last they find they have the treasure within them that they sought afar off.[8]

The experience of the soul.[9]

Now all is ardor and love; all earthly pleasures are not comparable to one moment of the joy the soul tastes. Its prayer is uninterrupted, becoming so ardent that it cannot contain it. Its senses (i.e., feelings or sensibilities) are so much spirit-centered, and its recollection in God so strong, that it longs to be in perpetual solitude with its Well-Beloved; for being not sufficiently established to be undisturbed by ordinary conversations, it is disposed to shun them.

---

[8] That is, "But when it was the good pleasure of God . . . to reveal his Son in me. . . ." (Galatians 1:15–16). Also, "The word is nigh thee, in thy mouth and in thy heart: that is, the word of faith, which we preach" (Romans 10:8). The writer is describing true conversion! "Repent . . . remission of your sins . . . *receive the gift of the Holy Spirit*" (Acts 2:38).

[9] The description now given coincides in many points with the "Way of Light." In both it describes what is really the "filling of the Spirit."

The Well-Beloved is so manifestly in possession that He rapidly reproves for an idle look or hasty word, and the soul changes more in one day than in years before. It seems as if sentinels were placed over all the senses, and as if it were no longer held to earth, so much does it feel detached therefrom.

The soul is so full of what it "feels" that it yearns to impart it to the whole world. Its words are all fire and flames, and it is fertile in beautiful thoughts; full of deep, lively feelings. All reasonings are swallowed up in ardent love, and one word from God awakens afresh the love that burns within.

The soul at this time experiences a vehement desire of suffering for Christ, and longs to satisfy Him. It is disposed to think itself at the summit of the spiritual life, and sees nothing more to be done than to enjoy (and give forth) the good it possesses.

> *Note:* This first degree of the "Way of Faith" lasts a long time, and there are many souls who, though admired of all mankind, do not go beyond it.

The secret faults in this degree.

The soul has a certain self-esteem, which is deeply hidden, and a secret contempt (i.e., "pity") for others not in its own experience. It is prone to be scandalized at their faults, and is *hard toward them.* It has a secret pride, so that it is troubled at faults committed openly—for it wants to be faultless.

It maintains a reserved bearing to others and claims to itself the gifts of God, forgetting its own weakness; it loses self-distrust, speaks rashly, and has a subtle desire to attract notice.

Although all these faults and many others are to be found deeply hidden, the person is unconscious of them, and even appears to have more humility than others, for at this stage one seems able to conceal his defects. If he falls into some visible fault he is beset with a swarm of self-reflections;[10] and when there comes any spiritual dryness he is dejected, discouraged and distressed, immediately believing that he has lost all. He then endeavors to do all he can to regain the presence of God.

He is so attached to his religious exercises that he prefers prayer to duty, and he is unyielding to those around. He is too ready to judge them, thinking it "a waste of time" to enter into their interests and give them pleasure. (See Romans 15:1–2.)

He observes austere silence at times, and at others is apt to talk without end about

---

[10]That is, thoughts dwelling upon self. One turns toward self instead of toward God for His searching and cleansing (1 John 1:9).

the things of God. He may, under the presence of obligation, impose upon himself unnecessary actions,[11] and thus fulfill his own will instead of the will of God.

The testings of this degree.

When dryness begins, the senses experience pain in remaining long in prayer—but the soul must be firm in not shortening its time of waiting upon God.

The strength of the soul is not equal to bearing such a trial for long, so that the Lord manifests Himself quickly again. He will gently teach it to let Him go and return without being disturbed.

After the intense joy of His manifested presence, the bereft soul is disposed to fight hard against His withdrawal, but in reality it is personal satisfaction in "owning" that it seeks; it loves for the pleasure of loving. *It is the "own" in its most subtle form in relation to Christ that now needs purifying.* The soul is willing to suffer, provided it has the manifested presence of the Well-Beloved, but it must learn to be faithful without any sign that He is pleased. It must be true without being so for reward!

---

[11]That is, "I *must* do this or that." Pliability to the slightest indication of God's will is needed, in order to walk faithfully with Him.

The believer honestly seeking to know God, and willing to be taught of Him, is soon caused to know wherein he comes short. He has no peace, even in peace itself, until he follows on to know the Lord. The torrent cannot rest short of the ocean. With the ceaseless cry after God, He leads the soul on, and it enters upon the next degree of the "Way of Faith."[12]

---

[12]Here it must be emphasized that while the soul is passing through the transition from the life of conscious fullness into the walk of pure faith—and the depth of calm of the life is wholly centered upon God, through all the painful alternations in experience, walking in obedience (1 Peter 1:2),—it must anchor upon the faithful God (Hebrews 6:17-19) and maintain its access to Him and communion with Him through the precious blood of Jesus. It is always "accepted in the Beloved" when it draws near in full assurance of faith (Hebrews 10:19-23). It will then be kept free from all "oppression of the enemy," and overcome him and all his accusations "because of the blood of the Lamb" (Revelation 12:10-11). Moreover as the soul is led on, by the Holy Spirit, from "faith unto faith" in the knowledge of God (Romans 1:17) and the Word of God effectually works to the dividing of soul and spirit (Hebrews 4:12), it must cast itself more and more, in faith, upon the life of Him who is a life-giving Spirit (1 Corinthians 15:45); for "we are become partakers of Christ, if we hold fast the beginning of our confidence firm unto the end" (Hebrews 3:14).

CHAPTER 2

THE WALK OF FAITH

The second degree in the "Way of Faith": frequent ups and downs. The third degree: the stripping of the soul, called "loss" or "burial."

THE SECOND DEGREE[1]

THE soul had been in such deep peace that it had no thought of ever losing it. It becomes inactive and ceases to advance. God has to move it on. He does this by withdrawing the old experience (Job 16:12; Job 29:2-3).

---

[1] This appears to consist at first of long or short periods of "dryness." Practically, it involves dealing with the emotional life, which at the beginning is much mixed with the *consciousness*, and *expression*, of spiritual things. The surrender of the excessive emotional life is necessary for the calm manifestation of the power of God; also for the sake of the earthen vessel and its sensitive organism, which is able to bear more strain in service when the emotions are not unduly called into use.

To the soul's astonishment, instead of maintaining its ground, the calm it thought it possessed forever seems gone, and the will appears powerless to gain control. Its emotional life is disturbed. A tumult begins in its waves!

At last it sees that its waves (emotions) were only hushed to sleep. It has now a better knowledge of itself, and for a time regains calmness.

After having received so many gifts from God, the soul thought it would remain in perpetual possession of them. To its grief it begins to experience an inclination for things it had left long ago. Distractions come in crowds, and it finds nothing but seasons of drought. The soul tries to regain its peace; tries to recover from its falls; it seeks solitude, hoping to find recovery there; it redoubles devotion, but all in vain. The fault seems to be its own and it tries to readjust things, but it cannot be done. At last it ceases from its own efforts and begins still further to know itself.

With the cessation of struggling, the Well-Beloved shows Himself again. How enraptured the soul is! It dreads to lose this new-found treasure again, the loss was so keen. It fears to displease Him, seeks to be more faithful, walks softly, *distrusts itself* more, and dreads the interruption of its peace.

The Walk of Faith / 29

This restored repose ravishes the soul, carries it away and makes it more neglectful (unwatchful). It cannot help yielding itself up to its delights, and wants to be alone to enjoy its joy! It is actuated now by a spiritual avidity or intemperance that disposes it to neglect duty. God must deliver it from this.

How spiritual self-absorption is dealt with.

The soul loses relish for prayer, and has the greatest difficulty in praying. Peace is again gone, and there is trouble deeper than ever.

Trials without multiply, while it appears more unable to endure them. It *tries* to be patient, but it weeps and is cast down (Job 16:16). It redoubles its cry after God, and can find no rest anywhere; it pants after God, yet He seems further away. He hides Himself to draw the soul out of itself after Him.

Oh, you who have never experienced these devices of love—lovely to the soul who has gone through them, terrible to the one that is under them—you have never learned deeply your weakness! This poor soul begins to lean no longer upon itself, but upon its Well-Beloved alone.

The soul becomes intensely sensitive to sin. Its knowledge of itself makes it wish to be reduced to powder, if that were possible! If a word against another seems wrong, what reparations it makes! It asks pardon as if it had committed a crime.[2]

The soul thinks it has caused the withdrawal of its Well-Beloved, yet does not cease to run after Him.

It has no relish for prayer, reading, or anything else, and service becomes difficult and burdensome. It dies to these things, inasmuch as they are done with such effort that they become a kind of death to it.[3]

At last it begins to see the profit of all this, and finds, after each manifestation of Christ, that the more it submits to the loss of all, the more purely He possesses it.

Understanding now intelligently the purpose of God, it gives itself up to "death" and agrees to the "comings and goings" of its Well-Beloved, when and how He wills. It

---

[2] It is easy to see the progress *downward!* There is no difficulty now in obeying "*first* be reconciled to thy brother" (Matthew 5: 24). It is the *selfhood* that finds it hard to stoop.

[3] Through this the soul learns to obey from principle, rather than from pleasant impulse. It *wills* to obey God and be faithful to duty. At this point the soul must take heed not to give occasion to the adversary by yielding to neglect of duty. In all its service it must not dwell upon its sense of powerlessness and emptiness, but cast itself upon God for His life to flow through its emptiness to others.

finds that its efforts to retain Him only hinder, and sees the object of His dealings. (See James 5:11.)

In this degree the further a soul advances, the shorter, purer, and simpler are its spiritual enjoyments, and the longer are its periods of "dryness" and trial, until it loses the its craving "to own," the appropriation or grasping of anything for itself. (Compare Matthew 10:39, Matthew 16:25, Luke 9:24.)

THE THIRD DEGREE

"If we have been grafted[4] into the likeness of His death, so shall we also share His resurrection" (Romans 6:5, *Conybeare*).

This may be called "loss" or "burial" (Romans 6:4–5), as the soul must be stripped of all, that it may find all in God.

It will be well to note that souls who are in the first degree do wrong to adopt the "rules" of more advanced stages. The "stripping" of the soul must be left to God. He will do so wisely and well if the person will but co-operate with Him. He impoverishes only to enrich, becoming in secret HIMSELF the substitute for all He takes away.

---

[4]Literally, *have become partakers of a vital union.* The meaning appears to be: *if we have shared the reality of His death, whereof we have undergone the likeness*—Conybeare's note.

Souls who have heard or read that they must be "stripped" often set about doing it themselves, and do not progress, for, as it is done by self-effort, God does not clothe them with Himself, which is His divine purpose in unclothing them.

In this stage the soul must not seek to sustain a life which has to be laid down. If we truly desire to live only in God we must not cling to, nor nourish, our life of "owning" in ever so little degree.[5] We must rest in the hand of the Faithful God, and let Him do as He wills.

Some souls are like drowning persons. They do not cease to resist[6] until they are exhausted. In pity God appears to be hard, and gives that soul no succor—so as to cause it to drop into the helplessness of

---

[5] Under the illumination of the divine Spirit, in charge of the soul, it continuously discerns two courses before it in the most ordinary actions of daily life. It is given to see how to co-operate with God by "hating" its own life, or how it may hinder His workmanship by nourishing itself in the most subtle ways.

[6] "There is a voluntary resistance which puts an absolute stop to the work of God, because He cannot violate man's freedom of will; there is also a resistance of nature—without being voluntary" (Madame Guyon). This may be the resistance of the feelings, or senses, and does not hinder His working if the *will* deliberately chooses to let Him have His way. "One may utter a cry because of these things" (See Job 30:24).

death. It ceases from its own works, and thereby enters into rest.

What is peculiarly afflicting at this time is that the pain always begins with something that appears to be one's *own fault!* At last the poor soul accepts its impotence, and despairs utterly of itself. It consents to the loss of all, and believes God has withdrawn all His gifts justly. When it sees another believer full of divine grace its pain is redoubled, and it is plunged into the deepest abasement.

The soul has no pleasure in anything; what avails anything to it now apart from God? It thinks it has lost Him or at least lost all its *love* of Him. It seems to itself so cold and ungrateful, but in truth it never loved Him or possessed Him more purely. It may have lost the emotion or vigor of love, but it has not lost HIM, and it must learn to love Him in Himself.

This does not mean that the senses do not turn at all towards the creature.[7] The soul knows this, and it constitutes its deepest grief, for it regards its involuntary faults

---

[7] That is, look to *others* for relief. "To help such a soul, very little relief should be given if the person concerned has tolerable strength of mind; otherwise it will be necessary to encourage and sustain. The less a strong and able soul is succored, the sooner will it learn to center wholly upon God."—Madame Guyon.

as dreadful transgressions.

THE STRIPPING OF THE SOUL

"Jehovah maketh poor, and maketh rich: He bringeth low, He also lifteth up" (1 Samuel 2:7).

God does not take away the spiritual riches except by *degrees*. The weaker the soul is the longer[8] He takes to strip it, and the stronger it is the sooner the work is finished. *Hard* as this stripping is, it is really only of outside things and superfluities.

He must take•away—

1. The ornaments (the gifts and graces).
2. The garments (the power for service).
3. The beauty (the power to practice divine virtues).

1. *The stripping of the ornaments.*

The Lord now removes all conscious experience of His grace and love. The soul is at first greatly afflicted, and sees the bad use it has made of His gifts and the self-complacency it has indulged in on account

---

[8]In faith and fixity of will. (See Job 13:15 as an example. Note Job's record of spiritual riches and his self-appropriation in Job 29, then the stripping and humiliation that followed in Job 30. Finally the restoration of all in Job 42:10–12.)

of them. Its sighs and its tears are the expression of its grief; then the Well-Beloved overwhelms it with new tokens of His love, which throws it into greater shame than ever. The soul hardly dares lift up its eyes, until it again forgets the past and sinks itself in these new favors of the Lord.

Some may ask, If the gifts of God are so hurtful, why impart them?

God gives them to draw the soul from sin to Himself. But the creature is so wretched as to make use of these very gifts for self-love and self-admiration. Self-love is so deeply implanted in the creature that these gifts serve to increase it, for *it finds in itself new charms* which did not before exist; it immerses itself into itself, clings to itself, appropriates to itself what belongs to God, and forgets out of what condition He has delivered it.

The soul stripped of its gifts from God loses something of its self-love, and begins to see that *nothing* belongs to it. ALL is God's. It sees that, as it has made wrong use of the gifts, it is better for God to keep them—and becomes glad that it has lost these things, because it sees the benefit of the loss.[9]

---

[9] The soul says, "I will be rich with the riches of my Well-Beloved" (see Colossians 1:29, Romans 8:32). "As having nothing, and yet possessing all things" (2 Corinthians 6:10).

2. *The stripping of the garments.*

After a time the Well-Beloved removes the old power for service; that is, so far as the consciousness is concerned, the *manifest* liberty and facility.

The case is worse than before! Though the soul had lost much, it could still freely perform its work. Now it resists with all its might: "This will bring reproach upon Thee," it cries. No matter. You must consent, poor soul; you do not yet know *yourself.* These very garments *pleased you,* and hindered you from seeing yourself.

The world begins to think less of it. They say, "Is *this* the person that was the admiration of all!" This unlooked-for revelation makes it still more distrustful of itself; it sees yet more how truly it has nothing of its own.

But it does not yet *hate* itself! Although stripped of graces (gifts and powers) it is still beautiful.

3. *The stripping of beauty.*

The soul has lost much, but it is able to practice the divine virtues. Now it must lose even these,[10] that is, as far as its "owned"

---

[10]That is, endurance as *endurance,* or a virtue apart from Christ. It loses the "virtue" as a possession, to possess it in Christ. See 1 Corinthians 1:30–31.

power to practice them is concerned. In reality, in the central depth, the divine life is deep and strong. This soul which so easily suffered all things finds now that it cannot endure anything! The exterior senses lose their submission, and seem to be in rebellion. It cannot guard itself as before.

It can do *nothing* by its own endeavors, as formerly it did, and it appears to itself to defile itself *every moment*.

It must, however, be said that a person brought to this condition by the inworking of the Holy Spirit does not commit voluntary (deliberate) faults. It must never be thought that *God* suffers the soul to fall into willful sin. He is granting it to see its corruption to the utmost, and it is overwhelmed with the holiness of God—a purity which makes it see the smallest mote of imperfection as enormous sin.[11]

The poor soul does not commit many of the faults it thinks it does. The truth is, the senses and faculties are without support; they therefore wander,[12] and to the sensi-

---

[11] Therefore the soul shelters continually under the blood sprinkled upon the Mercy Seat—the "blood of Jesus Christ" which "keeps cleansing" (lit.) from all sin (1 John 1:7).

[12] "Know that the effort which thou thyself mayest make to resist [wandering] thoughts is an impediment. The best thing . . . is sweetly to despise them . . . resign thyself . . . endure with patience, and persevere in [God's] presence."—Molinos.

tive heart this is terrible.

THE EXPERIENCE AT THIS STAGE

"He that HATETH his life [Gr. *psuche*, 'soul,' mg.—the life of the first Adam, see 1 Corinthians 15:45] in this world shall keep it unto life [Gr. *zoe*, the divine life] eternal" (John 12:25).

Now the soul truly *hates* itself. Yet all the knowledge that comes by *light* cannot make it really and actually loathe itself. (Compare this with the words of Job in Job 42:5–6.) If the soul is to know God, it must know its own misery apart from Him, and God searches out in that one's very depths what was most deeply hidden there. The grace of faith to permit stripping has always to do with the most deep-seated and hidden faults of the selfhood.

Moreover, the faults God searches out with His eyes of fire in the soul at this degree would pass as *virtues with others*—yes, others who have a thousand spiritual possessions they cherish dearly.

This soul has no longer anything at all. There is not left to it the least possession to glory in—nothing but weakness on weakness. Others live by something they *have*; this one lives by what he has NOT, for he has all in God. Accordingly he is far removed from attaching or attributing to himself anything.[13] ALL is of God, and he has nothing (2 Corinthians 6:10).

It must not be thought that the soul is forsaken of God, however wretched it feels; it was never more sustained by Him. It sees others full of divine grace, yet it does not envy them, so deeply does it feel its unfitness to have anything from God. It rejoices to see others thus filled, because they give the Well-Beloved joy. It is far from the jealousy of the first period. Moreover, it holds itself lowly in the presence of those whom it esteems happy in possessing the gifts of God.

The poor soul, having lost all it once possessed, must now *lose itself* by an utter despair of itself.

Prayer is difficult; the *imagination* seems in utter disorder, allowing scarcely any rest; the understanding, the memory, and the will appear to be without any power; it appears to have lost even God Himself (Job 23:8–9; Psalm 22:1–2; Psalm 88:14).

The soul has need to be very faithful in a time so hard. It should let itself lie in the

---

[13] This one can only say, "If I must needs glory, I will glory of the things that concern my weakness" (2 Corinthians 11:30). "I am nothing" (2 Corinthians 12:11).

40 / Life out of Death

hand of God, and patiently *endure itself*.[14]

God bears with it; He knew the depths of its corruption at the first. Why then should it not bear with itself?

It is now as *nothing* before God and others, and its self-hatred is such that it sees itself as worthy of all scorn. It is at last detached from all outward and *inward* possessions, for it has nothing to appropriate. It is

> "Circumcised with a circumcision not made with hands . . . having been buried with Him in baptism ["buried with Him through baptism into death," Romans 6:4] . . . through faith in the working of God" (Colossians 2:11–12).[15]

---

[14] Any disappointment with ourselves shows that we expected something from ourselves. To know what we *really are* in the sight of God means much stripping of veneer and much humiliation.

[15] This last degree is truly a passing through deep waters. "All Thy waves and billows have gone over me" is the cry of the faithful soul. But the Well-Beloved has said, "When thou passest through the waters I will be with thee; they shall not overflow thee" (Isaiah 43:2).

None can describe the tender upholding of His arms, and the strong, deep assurance He gives that His promise will be fulfilled to the obedient heart, in marvelous, unspeakable fullness.

"Yea, though I walk through the valley of deep darkness, I will fear no evil; for Thou art with me; Thy rod and Thy staff they comfort me" (Psalm 23:4, mg. See 1 Peter 4:19).

CHAPTER 3

THE NEW LIFE IN GOD

*Its characteristics. Its conditions.
What abandonment really means.*

THE FOURTH DEGREE

THIS is the divine and truly interior life, which contains degrees without number and in which the soul can make limitless advances. The torrent reaches the sea, and can evermore plunge deeper into the fathomless ocean.

All that has taken place hitherto has been within itself; now it is lifted out of itself to find a boundless capacity in God.

Life Abundant. Ceasing from itself, the soul becomes conscious of a new force[1]

---

[1] It appears to the soul as if a "new force" and "new life" were taking possession, but in reality it is only the *new consciousness* of a life that has been deepening day by day, as the faithful heart pressed on to know the Lord.

taking possession of it—a silent power taking control and pervading its whole being. It is entering into life that springs out of death, a life with Christ in God.

Those who think themselves in this degree but who are yet straitened and powerless are not in true resurrection life, for that means that the soul is restored both to *life* and the *actions of life*. In this present, spiritual resurrection everything is restored a hundredfold (Mark 10:29–30), together with increasing facility in its use, without an appropriating of anything to oneself as before.

THE CHARACTERISTICS OF THE LIFE OF UNION

The soul is possessed by God.

It possesses no longer; it is *possessed*. God being the principle of life cannot want for anything. The soul has lost the created for the Creator; nothingness for all things (Colossians 2:9–10).

The soul has all things in God.

It lives no longer, works no longer of *itself*. It is God Himself (by the Holy Spirit) who lives, works, operates within it. This goes on increasingly, so that it becomes rich with His riches, loving with *His* love. This is so by degrees as it was stripped by degrees (2 Corinthians 3:18). All is given back to it in God, not to be owned by itself, but in Him (1 Corinthians 3:21–23).

The soul lives without effort.

The divine life possessing it and working in it works with the same unconscious ease as the natural life.[2] It no longer thinks about itself, and how it acts. It gives itself freely to the duty of the moment, leaving to its Possessor the care of working in it, to will and to do of His good pleasure (Philippians 2:13; Hebrews 8:10–11).

The soul is in perfect rest.

It is wholly satisfied in God. It is possessed by the peace of God, therefore its peace is unchangeable (Philippians 4:7). It abides in Him restfully, without troubling about itself. It does not question within itself whether it is recollected or wandering, whether it is this or that; for it does not think about itself.

It is not necessary to retire within to find God, for the soul does not seek Him there any more.[3] If one were surrounded by the

---

[2] Note the effortless growth of the lilies, a suitable picture of this (Matthew 6:28).

[3] He *is* there; but the soul does not *seek* Him there, because He is everywhere. He is within and without; above and around (Acts 17:28).

sea there could be no choice of one part more than another; the only need would be to abide in the environment.

The soul has a boundless joy.

Nothing can disturb the peace or lessen the joy, though the latter is not sensibly perceived. It is a joy unspeakable (1 Peter 1:8), God having strengthened the soul to bear it.

The soul is in harmony with the divine will.

It has no separate will,[4] for its will is the will of God; it has no desire but to fulfill His desires; for it has lost all repugnance and contrariety towards the will of God.

The soul is bought into simplicity.

Its condition of life has become so simple that it has nothing to say about itself. (See Matthew 10:16, mg.; 2 Corinthians 11:3.) It is silent, not because of reserve, but because its experience passes all expression by its extreme simplicity. There are no vi-

---

[4]This does not mean an extinct will, but a will that is brought into harmony with the divine will so as to freely, gladly, and spontaneously will the will of God above all things.

sions, revelations, ecstasies, or changes in this degree of divine life. It is above all these, for this way is simple, seeing nothing except as in God, the ONE center and principle of all things, and environed by Him.

All distinction in service is taken away. The meanest service and the (so-called) highest are alike beautiful to it if but in the divine will;[5] therefore souls of this degree do not covet great things for themselves, being content to be in the will of God each moment.

The soul is one with Christ in God.

God is no longer distinct from the soul; it is in God as in the atmosphere natural to it. It is no longer *conscious* of love, light, or knowledge. It only knows that *God is*, and that it no longer lives but in Him. It no more "feels" Him than we feel the air we breathe. The soul finds itself clothed with the inclinations of Christ, not knowing how; not by distinct views of Him, or seeking to copy

---

[5] There is no shrinking from duty for prayer, nor from prayer for actual service. God meets the soul in all things that come in His will. Circumstances, and the duties of life, *are* in His providential will; souls in God find God in all. "The highest love to God does not require us to violate our duty to our neighbor, or even to our enemy. When our religious experience stops in 'emotionality' it is apt to do this."—Upham's *Life of Madam Guyon*.

Him, but by finding these dispositions—the outcome of His life—manifested in humility, submission, etc., just as, and when, circumstances require.

Its treasure is now God alone, from whom it draws continually all its needs (Colossians 1:19; 2 Corinthians 9:8).

THE APOSTOLIC LIFE

In this degree the apostolic life begins,[6] the life of abundant fruitfulness. Many are directed to these souls, to whom these ones communicate *life* (2 Corinthians 2:16), thereby winning many to Christ. This life-power flows spontaneously, and without thought of "carefulness" on the part of the vessel (John 7:38).

Liberty

This is the degree in which true liberty is given, and great *facility* and *power* for doing all things in the order of God.[7]

Nothing that God desires the soul to do is now difficult. If He calls to preach, or teach,

---

[6] Its characteristics can easily be traced in the apostles after Pentecost, and, more in detail, in the life of the Apostle Paul.

[7] "Whatever is in the order and value of God, expands it; everything else contracts it, and this contraction restrains it from passing out."—Madame Guyon.

there is marvelous facility, for He is the source of it all (1 Corinthians 2:13).

It may be noted that this wonderful facility is not always given at *first*, and often not until after an experience of powerlessness. It is important not to force oneself in these matters, and to be careful not to go beyond the measure of God's gift (Ephesians 4:7; 2 Corinthians 10:13).

Power

The soul in God has great power over others with whose interests it is charged by God—but all *outside of itself*. Others are no longer a "trial" to it, because its heart enlarges every day to contain them. (See 2 Corinthians 6:11–12.)

Illumination

In these souls the secrets of God are revealed, not by word, sight, or *light*, but by an inward principle, the principle of knowing God. (See 1 Corinthians 2:9–13.) When the soul writes or speaks, it is itself astonished to find that all flows from a divine center. In the manifestation to others, it sees the revelation to itself. It is surprised to find itself writing of things it knew not before. It was not so in other degrees; there the light preceded experience: here experience precedes light.

All in this degree have God possessing them, according to their capacity. All are *full*, but not all have an equal amount of fullness. It seems a contradiction to say the soul must pass into God and yet to speak of a capacity that remains, but such is the case.

There are two kinds of capacity, one belonging to the creature, small and limited; the other a capacity in God, a capacity of being lost more and more in Him.

The stripping and melting process through which the person has passed has taken from him all form (which compressed him within the rigid limit of his own capacity), and disposes him to flow into God, as water joined to its source blends with it ever deeper and deeper. (This does not mean that he loses his nature as a creature, and that God could not cast him forth again—although this is what He will not do.)

The soul is so free, and so large, that the whole earth appears but a point to it. It is free to do all things and to do nothing. It can adapt itself to any condition and circumstance. It is no longer narrowed, limited, or confined as regards anything (cf. Philippians 4:12–13).

THE EARTHEN VESSEL

"I, Paul . . . in outward appearance, am base among you" (2 Corinthians 10:1, mg., KJV).

"God chose . . . the base things of the world, and the things that are despised" (1 Corinthians 1:27–31).

The *exterior* is very ordinary, and the soul has nothing to distinguish it from others. There is nothing externally apparent except to those to whom it is sent with a divine message. God hides the soul in His bosom and from the world, under the veil of a most ordinary life.

Suffering. As the soul is strong, strengthened by Himself, God gives it more trials, and heavier ones than before, but it bears them with His divine power of endurance (Philippians 4:13; Colossians 1:24).

The senses (feelings) suffer pain and remain subject to suffering,[8] but the central depth of the soul retains its equanimity because He who possesses it is immutable. There would appear to be a separation of

---

[8] This is true in a much *keener* degree the more the life of God is realized. Sin *dulls* the sensibilities; consequently the more the soul is delivered from the power of sin and the life of the selfhood, the more it is capable of fellowship with Him of whom it is written, "He . . . *suffered* being tempted" (Hebrews 2:18).

the two parts, the higher and the lower: they live together like strangers who do not know each other. No pain prevents the perfect peace, tranquility, joy and immovableness of the higher part, as the divine condition of the higher does not hinder extreme suffering in the lower. (See 2 Corinthians 1:5.) The cessation is not of suffering, but of the sorrow, anxiety and bitterness of suffering.

Faults. The faults of a soul at this stage are more subtle than formerly. It knows them better because it has its eyes open! It must not make endeavors to cleanse itself; the effort would add to the sin.[9] It must abide in its rest in God, trusting Him to free it from all sin that He continues to reveal (Philippians 3:15; 1 John 1:7).

All thought of *return* must be put aside, because to *return* presupposes having gone away from Him; and the soul must continue to abide in Him.

THE CONDITIONS OF ABIDING

"If ye keep My commandments, ye shall

---

[9]"When we fall into error, and even undoubted sins, simply in deep humiliation and penitence turn calmly and believingly, *without fear and agitation*, to Him who forgives willingly; to that cross of Christ where wounded souls are healed."—Upham's *Life of Madam Guyon.*

abide in My love" (John 15:10).

"Thou standest by thy faith. Be not highminded, but fear" (Romans 11:20).

Faithful co-operation with God. The soul must give itself up to God, every moment to be possessed and controlled by Him. Faithfulness consists *not* in a passive inaction (a powerless negation) but in doing nothing except through the divine life by which it is animated[10] (Colossians 1:29).

Acceptance of the will of God every moment. It must receive the events of Providence (i.e., every circumstance of the day) each moment as the will of God for that moment, without regretting the past or anticipating the future.

Avoidance of self-reflection. If the soul never *looked at itself* what advances it would make! The thinking of self should be shunned above all else; it is the one thing that leads the soul back into itself—and this is always possible, whatever degree it may have reached. It is stopped from progress as long as its self-reflection continues. (When it does relapse into itself this does not mean that it goes out of its *degree*, but only out of the divine movement.)

---

[10]Note the words of the Lord Jesus, "He that speaketh from himself seeketh his *own* . . . he that seeketh the glory of [God] . . . the same is true" (John 7:18. Compare also John 5:30, John 6:38).

Avoidance of self-effort. It must leave to God the originating[11] of occasions, and simply walk in the path He prepares for it.

The soul may not act of itself even in ever so small a measure without being guilty of unfaithfulness. The soul can force itself to act contrary to the inward instruction. *Absolute inability* is not what God has promised. In the divine life it has facility for all that lies in the path of duty, and in obedience to the will of God.[12]

GOD ALL IN ALL

"Our fellowship is with the Father, and with His Son Jesus Christ" (1 John 1:3).

"Even as Thou, Father, art in Me, and I in

---

[11]The movement of God in the soul will be met by the corresponding movement of God in providence. This is the exterior "witness" to the God-given interior prompting which is never contrary to or *beyond* what is written. (See 1 Corinthians 4:6.) The soul is not to originate but to co-operate with the working of God. That is to say, it is to watch for the movings of God in exterior things and work with Him, as He works in it and around it. This leaves no room for the "push" of the creature, and cuts away much fruitless "work," while it enables the Creator to fulfill His highest purpose for His redeemed creation. (Compare Hebrews 13:21, mg.)

[12]*Obedience up to light* is one of the main conditions of "abiding," to which may be added *faith* in the faithfulness of God to maintain the soul in Him, and, as well, the Word of God, dwelling richly in the heart, and the continuous application by the Holy Spirit of the blood of sprinkling (1 Peter 1:2).

Thee, that they also may be in Us . . . that they may be one, even as We are one" (John 17:21–22).

The soul is lost in God with Jesus Christ. All around it is God. It is now so "rooted and fixed in God" that it is as an immovable rock, not to be shaken by trials or blows of any kind (Acts 20:24). God puts it to strange testings, and He does not leave it the shadow of anything to cling to or rest upon, out of *Himself*.[13]

Here all is God;[14] God is everywhere, and

---

[13] The writer points out that souls do not reach the *consummation* of the fourth degree as quickly as they think; the most spiritual person is apt to mistake the maturity of the "Way of Light" for this. She says also that many know it transitorily previous to being established in it, because God gives in the first place the light of it and then a foretaste, afterwards withdrawing the conscious knowledge of it that He may work out the reality, finally restoring the assurance of the life in God. As the soul follows on to know the Lord, and the divine light is intensified, the further it advances the more it is disposed to say, "Not that I have already obtained . . . but I press on . . . toward the goal unto the prize of the upward calling of God in Christ Jesus" (Philippians 3:12–14, mg.).

[14] The First Epistle of John seems written from this standpoint. Note John's frequent expression, "*of God*" (1 John 4: 4–6, etc.), and "*in God*" (1 John 4:15–16). "God abideth in him, and he in God." See the Lord's words in John 3:21, mg., "Works . . . made manifest, because they have been wrought *in God*."

in all things (2 Corinthians 5:18); and thus the soul is equal in all. Its prayer is always equal and never interrupted (1 Thessalonians 5:17), although the soul does not perceive it except by its unbroken peace; if, at times, God diffuses some overflowing of His glory over its senses, it makes no change in the central depth, which continues the same.

The torrent is now in the ocean and has the ebb and flow of the sea—moving with God and in God, in restful correspondence with His movements. It is the sea that carries it along, and it can make boundless advances.

WHAT IS TRUE ABANDONMENT?

How many make terms with God, and put limits as to how far they will submit to His doings! This is abandonment in figure, not in reality. Entire abandonment excepts nothing, reserves nothing. But how many will submit to lie in the hand of their Creator, leaving to Him full power to treat them as He will, making no resistance and caring not what the world will say?

What do you fear, O craven heart? You are afraid of losing yourself! Considering how little you art worth, what great matter is that? Yes, you will lose yourself if you will abandon yourself to God, but you will lose yourself *in Him*.

Alas, people are so blind. They consider this as unsuitable for great minds. It is something too low for them. This path is very little known because most are so wise and prudent. It is "hidden . . . from the wise and prudent, and . . . revealed . . . unto babes" (Matthew 11:25, *KJV*).

By what route does God lead to Himself? By ways quite opposite to those we should imagine for ourselves. He builds up by casting down. He gives life by taking it away. Oh life, how narrow is the way that leads to thee! Oh love, thou art purest of all—for thou art God Himself!

Oh blessed nothingness, how glorious is Thy consummation; what gain, oh my soul, hast thou not made for all thy losses! Thou art

LIFTED ABOVE ALL BY THE LOSS OF ALL.

CHAPTER 4

CHARACTERISTICS OF A SOUL IN DIVINE UNION

Extracted and summarized from *Divine Union in the Higher Forms of Religious Experience,* by T. C. Upham, D.D.

TO WHATEVER degree we approach quietness of spirit we also approach similitude to God.

The man who moves unshaken in the sphere and path which God has marked out for him, unelated by joy, undepressed by sorrow, unallured by temptation, unterrified by adversities, this man bears always the calm of his Elder Brother and is truly God-like.

1. *The soul in union rests from reasoning.*

It is difficult for a man, so far as he is in alienation from God, to suppress reasoning. He reasons because he has lost the God of reason. When God is displaced from

His proper position of centrality, the relations of truth as the subject of one's perceptions are entirely unsettled and thrown out of balance.

The truly renewed soul has rest from the vicious and perplexing reasoning of nature. The true wisdom is to wish to know all that God would have us know; to employ our perception and reasoning faculty under a divine guidance; and to seek nothing beyond that limit.

Oh, you who are seeking for the truth, having exercised your reason till you find there is no peace in it—rest in the God of reason! What you know not, God knows. Blindfolded, walk on with God's hand to guide you. He will work out problems for the humility of faith—revealing solutions which He hides from unsanctified deduction.

2. *The soul in union rests from all desires that do not harmonize with the will of God.*

There are two classes of desires—those that spring from an unsanctified nature and those which are from God. Agitation and sorrow attend the one and true peace the other. In God is the fulfillment of our desires. In God, therefore, there is rest.

3. *The soul in union rests from the re-*

proofs of conscience.

Souls in partial union, going through the transition stages, have constant conflict in themselves. They see the right but continue in some degree to follow the wrong. They are constantly the subject, more or less, of inward admonition. But conscience has its smiles as well as its frowns! The renovated soul rests from the *condemnation* of conscience.

The constraints of conscience precede action. The reproofs of conscience follow action. The soul in union does right without constraint. He has freely given himself to God to be moved by Him, and God moves him by making him a partaker of the divine nature. Such a one may be said to act by nature and not by constraint, by a life *moving it at the center* and not by compulsive instigation—which has no higher office than to guard and compel the center. It is unnecessary to drive a person who goes without driving.

4. *The soul in union rests from all disquieting fears.*

He is delivered from fear of want, fear of suffering, fear of man, and guilty fear of God. The fear which is based upon guilt is very different to that fear which is synonymous with reverence.

5. *The soul in union rests from conflict with providence.*

The soul united to God is necessarily united with Him in all the movements and arrangements which He makes. He rests from the perplexities of making this or that decision by accepting the choice his Father makes for him in all circumstances. God's choice is only another name for His providence.

Moreover, God's providence is internal as well as external. He is the Inspirer of the feelings of the heart as well as the Director of outward events. The renewed soul therefore rests from all anxiety as to the particular form of his inward experience; he rests from vain and wandering imaginations, and from mentally returning to other scenes and situations in unholy discontent. He rests from feelings of envy which suppose the existence of superiority in others, in position or anything else. He rests from easily offended feelings; if injured by another, he knows that his Father (who never originates the unholy impulse) has seen fit for some wise reason to direct its application against himself. He receives the blow with a quiet spirit, while he has sorrow for him who inflicts it.

6. *The soul in union rests from labor.*

The term *labor* implies effort. There is life and activity in heaven, but not labor—which involves pain and effort. The soul renovated does not cease to be active, for he finds and knows no idle moments; but the work which he does ceases to possess the ordinary attributes of labor, because (a) *there is a divine power working in him,* (b) *his activity is inspired by love.*

The labor of the partially sanctified man who stirs himself to action by reasonings, reflections, and the forced efforts of the will is not the recreation and happiness of the soul in union. The latter person works without knowing that he works. Love converts what would otherwise be work into the spontaneous activity of the life within him. In doing what he loves to do, he labors just as much as the birds do when they fly and sing.

In saying, therefore, that the renewed soul rests from labor we do not mean that he rests from action, but the action is so easy, so harmonious with the desires of the soul, so in accord with the arrangements of Providence, that there is no pain or distaste in labor. The divine life acts by innate disposition; it merely needs opportunities of action and not instigation to action.

7. *To the soul in union are expressions applied which seem to be directly opposite to each other in their import.*

(a) *"He is dead, and is alive again."* That is to say, dead to private aims, interests, selfish passion, prejudices and pleasures; to worldly reputation and honor. He is alive to God and His interests; to the honor which comes from God and from God only.

(b) *"He is without action, and yet always acting."* That is to say, he is always in harmony with Providence—moving as he is moved upon: retreating, going forward, or standing still, just as the voice of God in the soul directs. Action is as essential to him as life; but it is action *in God* and *for God*.

(c) *"He is always suffering, and yet always happy."* The opposition between the peace of his own soul and things around him causes affliction, but in the inward recesses of the soul faith stands unshaken. It is a faith which proclaims a present God, so he is always happy.

(d) *"He is ignorant, and feels himself to be so, and yet is full of divine wisdom."* He can say sincerely, "I know nothing," because human knowledge compared with the divine is always ignorance; but if he has no knowledge from himself he still has God for his teacher.

(e) *"He is poor and yet he has all riches."*

Characteristics of a Soul in Divine Union / 63

Poor because he has nothing he can call his own. That which the world calls *his*, he calls *God's!* He is a poor son with a rich Father.

(f) *"He is weak, and yet has all power."* He has renounced his own strength; he has no power in himself, yet he has all power in God.

8. *The soul in union has peace, because his action is natural.*

A natural life is that life which develops itself in accordance with the principles of its own nature, and which, in doing so, is true and harmonious to itself. The divine life established in the soul works in the same "natural" way as the life of nature.

The person in union easily adapts himself to the demand of the moment in the providence of God. While the inward fountain of love is always the same, and always full, the streams which flow from it are either repelled by opposition or attracted by sympathy.

Such a soul remains in union with the divine nature even though there is *diversity in manifestation.* Under the impulses of the life from God he becomes all things to all men without losing the identity of his character as a child of God. He can sit at meat with sinners or receive the hospitality of the

Pharisees, and in both cases he will unite the propriety of love with the faithfulness of duty. In his simplicity he is the companion of children; and in his wisdom the counselor of age.

All this seems to imply contradiction and to require effort, but its ease and promptness is the working of a divine life within. This absence of effort has sometimes perplexed even those who have been led by the Holy Spirit into the higher forms of experience. The suggestion arises in their minds—since the perception of their own working is lost in the fact of God's working—that perhaps nothing has been done at all. They doubt because all is so easy and natural. Yet the life of God operates much in the same way as does instinct in the lower animals; they move as they are moved, by an instinctive power within them.

9. *The soul in union has passed from meditation to contemplation.*

The contemplative is naturally preceded by the meditative. In the definite and formal act of the will, meditation, in order to render the mental operation more easy and effective, is understood to require a time and place set apart.

Meditation, though necessary, is not altogether a natural condition. It implies a degree of effort, and of resistance against other forces, and does not appear to be consistent with the higher rest and peace of the soul.

Contemplation, in contrast, is a calm dwelling upon God in thought, with affectionate exercises of the heart. It differs from meditation in several points:

(a) The object in both is God; but in contemplation the heart is not propelled towards its object by an effort of the will, but is rather attracted towards it with a sweet quietude of spirit.

(b) In meditation the mind dwells upon a God local, so to speak, dwelling upon a throne. This conception of God is well suited to earlier stages—and there is truth in it, as far as it goes, but not the whole truth; for God occupies place, but is not *limited* to place. When our conception expands in some degree to the magnitude of its object, we find God not in form or place *only*, but in *all* places—and He is still a personal God.

The meditative man attaches himself to the God local; the contemplative man to the God *universal*. To seek God in a place requires a degree of effort. To commune with Him in all places and among all objects is natural and easy, because we contemplate Him always as a God *present*. Being in the midst of places and objects, none of which can separate us from the divine Presence, all the soul has to do is to look and love. Calmly and sweetly it looks upon every object, and finds itself dwelling upon God who created all.

In the higher degrees, contemplation becomes almost permanent. It may be broken briefly by pressure of care, or business, but it becomes the natural disposition of the soul.

Quietness of spirit in this degree is the sign of truth, of rectitude of spirit, and of a right course of action. On the other hand, a spirit disturbed, in a state of agitation, is the sign of a wrong done, or of a wrong proposed to be done. Accordingly, in any proposed course of action, if it cannot be entered upon in entire quietness of spirit— with one's soul entirely calm—then the probability is that the course is wrong, or at least doubtful, and is safely delayed until there is further light.

To him who has this deeper insight and is in this higher unity, God breathes in all things; all inanimate nature is full of Him, the All in all. He sees God in what is ordinarily called the work of men's hands. It is God who spreads his pillow; God who builds his house. He sees God in all the changes that take place around him. All things are His, sin only excepted; sin *is* sin because it is *not* of God.

The man who rests in God by being brought into harmony with the divine nature cannot be restricted by the limitation of name or country; he has a spirit which belongs to the world. A divine peace is written upon his heart, his countenance, his actions, his whole life. He sees the commotions of the world, but they do not move him nor alter the fixedness of his purpose and the calm of his spirit. He is not indifferent to the strife, but he knows the God who has power to control it, and he therefore sees the calm beyond.

CHAPTER 5

FOUR PLANES OF THE SPIRITUAL LIFE

THERE are four planes—broadly speaking—in the spiritual life of the believer, and of the Christian worker.

The first plane we may call the *evangelistic* plane: that is, the plane where the soul knows the new birth, knows that he has eternal life in Christ; where also he becomes a soul-winner, preaches salvation from the penalty of sin, and is used to lead others to Christ; where the entire objective is winning souls for Christ and where he is faithful in proclaiming the gospel of salvation in Christ.

Then there is the second plane, which may be called the *revival* plane—the stage in personal experience where the believer receives the fullness of the Holy Spirit; where he learns to know Him and to obey Him, to rely upon Him and to look to Him to work as he co-operates with Him, and is used to lead others into the experience of the fullness of the Spirit.

Then there is the third plane, which we may call the plane of the *path of the cross,* where the believer experientially apprehends his position in Romans 6 in fellowship with Christ's death; where he is brought into "conformity" to His death (Philippians 3:10), learns the fellowship of His sufferings, and is led to walk in the path of the cross in every detail of practical life. Here the believer is able to interpret to others the way of the cross, and to lead others to know Romans 6 and 2 Corinthians 4:10–12 in experience.

The fourth plane is the plane of *spiritual warfare.* It is really the "ascension" plane, where the believer knows his union with Christ, seated with Him "far above all principality and power" (Ephesians 1:21, KJV); and where, in service, he is in aggressive warfare against the powers of darkness; learns to have spiritual discernment to detect the working of the devil; and learns the authority of Christ over all the power of the enemy (Luke 10:19).

Or to put it concisely—the first is the plane of *salvation,* or the new life; the second is the plane of the *Spirit;* the third is the plane of *victory over sin;* the fourth is the plane of *victory over the powers of dark-*

ness.

The individual *believer*, if he goes forward in the Christian life with God, is generally—not *always*—led just in this order also. First, he receives salvation; second, he receives the Holy Spirit in His fullness; third, he is led along the path of the cross; fourth, he walks in the path of conflict and victory, resulting in "authority" (Luke 10:19, *NIV*, Ed.) over all the power of the enemy. The individual *worker*, also, finds he is used in these four planes of service. First, he is used to lead others to Christ; second, he is used to lead them into the fullness of the Spirit; third, he is used to interpret to them the path of the cross; and fourth, he is enabled to discern the devices and workings of the devil, and to have authority over "all the power of the enemy" through union with Christ on the throne.

Madame Guyon truly says that in every plane of the spiritual life there is a beginning, a working out, and a consummation of the life in that degree, followed by a passage into the next plane, where there is again a beginning, a working out, a consummation. In each plane you appear to learn the very same lessons over again, but they are all being learned in a deeper degree. For instance, in the first plane you learn the way of faith in Christ as Saviour, and then you have to learn to exercise faith again in the next plane, and again in the next. It is just as hard to learn the lesson of bare faith in the fourth plane as in the first, and yet, as you look back, you can see the hard lessons of the first plane are now quite simple and easy.

Further, it is true that, speaking generally, it often takes years to get through each plane! When you pass into a new plane of the spiritual life, it is often with some great conscious "blessing"—a God-given experience of fullness in Christ, which may be described as a "taste" of what God has for you in that plane in its consummation. For instance, you get a revelation of the ascension life—being seated with Christ in the heavenly places—and the joy and light of it is so real that you think you will never come down again to the lower planes you now leave behind you; but in a brief while of weeks, or months, the conscious blessing—lasting according to the extent of the revelation and its power—apparently disappears, and you perhaps struggle to regain what you think you have lost. Now you have to fight by bare faith to hold the ground you have taken. Then follows what may be called a "tunnel" experience, when you go through test upon test; in which, perhaps, you may think you fail, but through all you find there is *advancement*, and final em... into the full consummation of that specific plane of the spiritual life, where you understand the way of abiding. For in the working into you of that life by the "tunnel" experience, God has removed what stands in the way of the permanent abiding in that stage of the knowledge of Him. (See Romans 5:2–5.)

But let us remember, if God gives you a message which He means you to take hold of, *He holds you*, even when you appear to lose it. His message given to you *lays hold of you*. That word has divine life and energy in it, and it can grip you, and hold you to it. God requires your co-operation, of course, and you must actively take the word by faith; but the power is in the word itself when God has spoken it to you. If the Lord has given you the word "authority over the power of the enemy," you have to co-operate by saying in response, "I *choose* and accept it, Lord, but I have no power to hold it; the word must hold me."

And in truth you often apparently lose it, so that it goes right away from you; but if you go on steadily in bare faith, you come at last through the tunnel-working of God to the consummation point, and then what looked like a literal impossibility to you when God gave you the light you find has been wrought into you as part of your very life—assimilated and incorporated into your spiritual being.

When a believer has pressed on with God faithfully from plane to plane, and has reached the sphere of warfare and victory over the powers of the air, then he should be able to lead others into any of the degrees of blessing they need; but, usually, when the soul is in a certain stage, and has not arrived at its full consummation, he can only help others in the same stage, speaking out of his present light and experience. It is not until the consummation point is reached that the believer has liberty and facility in dealing with others in planes which he himself has left behind. In the transitional stage of each plane you can give only the *vision* you have, so that your ministry seems limited to those who are at the same stage. You interpret to them what you, *and they*, are experiencing. But when you are *through that plane*, it seems as if you are able to minister to souls at any degree as they may need it.

Therefore you must never be disturbed if anyone says that your "message" did not help them at all, for possibly your message was "above their heads." The fact is, you were obliged to give it, for you were not free enough for anything else, and you ministered only to a certain number of souls who could be helped by that message.

What about others? you ask. Remember, you cannot meet the needs of all until you have passed through the *stages* of all. A worker needs to be very matured in the spiritual life to have light and truth for "all saints," just as Paul had, and the other apostles.

When the believer has passed through these "planes"—a matter of years, more or less—and he reaches the plane of power over the forces of darkness in its fullest degree, then he is in the "apostolic" stage—with sufficient facility and equipment and knowledge and liberty, from his own experience of the Word of Righteousness (Hebrews 5:13), to be able to handle the Word of God as a steward, and to minister it to others at their various degrees. When you become matured and ripened, then you do not speak from what you yourself are at the moment experiencing, but you are able to use the Scripture of truth as an armory, and be "furnished completely" for every good work, able to wield or apply the Word of God to each soul. This is real equipment, and ripeness of maturity, and fitness for service in the power of the Holy Spirit.

What is also needed is that Christians should know that the victory of Calvary over the powers of darkness is required to be apprehended by them in every stage of the spiritual life, and every plane of experience. (1) *The evangelist needs to know it,* because to win souls to Christ he must learn how to bind the devil holding souls; and therefore the truth of victory over the powers of darkness as declared in the Word of God is part of the evangelist's armor and equipment. (2) *Those who receive the baptism of the Holy Spirit* need to know the victory over the powers of darkness, so as to be able to detect the counterfeits, and to refuse them. (3) *Those who go on in the path of the cross* equally need to know the devices of the deceiving spirits, because they will interfere with them at every step onward in their knowledge of the cross and try to mix their workings with the work of God in every degree. In fact, the truths about the powers of darkness need to be known in every plane, and at each stage of the spiritual life, according to the measure and need.

But the urgent work to be done now is to meet the need of *the advanced ranks of the church of Christ:* those who can "by reason of use"—i.e., as the result of practice—exercise their spiritual senses, and are able to "eat" and assimilate the "solid food" which is for those of full age; who also can give the

Four Planes of the Spiritual Life / 7

same spiritual food in "milk" form to the babes, so that they may grow (see Hebrews 5:13–14).

If, in helping others, you find that believers do not understand the meaning of the prayer-warfare, you should ask them if they know anything about the cross, and the position of death with Christ according to Romans 6; for they must know the death to sin and to the world *before they can understand the spiritual warfare.* If they do not know the power of the cross, you must go further back and ask them if they know the *baptism of the Holy Spirit,* for the power to know experientially the fellowship of Christ's death is given by the Holy Spirit. If they do not know the baptism of the Holy Spirit, you must go further back still, and ask them if they possess the new life in Christ at all. How can a soul receive the fullness of the Holy Spirit if it does not know Christ as a Saviour, and is not born from above into the kingdom of Christ? We must as workers be able to lead souls back from point to point to the place of need, and recognize the four grades, or planes, of growth in dealing with them.

For these who already know the baptism of the Spirit and the path of the cross, *the pressing need is light on the warfare with Satan;* but another need on a wider scale is

...riential knowledge of the baptism ...oly Spirit, for a vast number of believers do not know this and the two-fold aspect of the cross. Therefore they cannot understand what we mean by "warfare" and the need of the discerning of spirits. It is not enough to proclaim victory over the powers of darkness; you must lead the children of God to know the cross in its relation to believers. The warfare of Ephesians 6 is a spiritual warfare, and only through the death of the cross is the believer brought into the spiritual realm, and the conflict there.

Many Christians are perplexed over receiving the Holy Spirit because they think they only have the proof of having done so *if they have manifestations of His presence:* so on this subject many questions arise. The Scriptures make it clear that you receive Him by faith (Galatians 3:2–3), but there is a succeeding work to be done in real surrender to obey Him, and the putting of all obstacles out of the way of His fullest working. The hindrances to His working through the believer must be removed, and the wrong things in the life put away, as revealed progressively by Him.

When does the special need of light on the powers of darkness and their workings now come in? All over the world there are large numbers of believers definitely and clearly preaching full assurance of salvation in Christ. There are also an increasing number of believers who really know the baptism of the Holy Spirit, and are in the "revival" plane, or the plane of knowing the Holy Spirit and co-working with Him. Again there are others—a smaller company—knowing the Holy Spirit, who have really pressed on in the power of the Spirit to follow the Lamb of Calvary in the path of the cross.

Now speaking generally, these last-named believers are blocked, because they have no glimmer of anything beyond this. They have thought that they have simply to go on to the end in the path of the cross—in the Spirit of the Lamb. Meanwhile, the powers of darkness have been coming in like a flood to the church of Christ, blocking and hindering the work of God on every side. The message needed by these souls who know the fellowship of the cross—the crucified life—is the knowledge of the aggressive war upon the powers of darkness. The call to these is, "*Arise*, in the new life of Christ, and in the equipment of the Holy Spirit—whom you have already known to lead you unto death—and lay hold of *the victory of Christ* and move aggressively against the foe." These, having died to the old fleshly life of activity (the soulish life energy), having died to the world and become separated into Christ—*these are the souls who need to see their union with Christ in the ascension life, and His authority over all the power of the enemy.*

Here we must point out a cause of danger in the life of many who know the path of the cross. They have learned the power of the Holy Spirit and also the path of the cross—they have understood that they were to "follow the Lamb," to *submit* to the will of God, and they have followed on in that path faithfully—until now they may have unknowingly gone on a point too far. Their "surrender" may have become "passivity"—i.e., a passive condition of mind, and sometimes of all their faculties—which is not according to God. Having ceased to "resist" in the "flesh" they have sunk into a passive submission to all things around them, not only to the "will of God" but to the will of Satan, and failed in their attitude of resistance "in the spirit" to the spiritual foe! Their surrender to "the will of God" became, or has become unconsciously, a *passive submission* to Satan. There has undoubtedly come upon the church a heavy pressure of the powers of darkness, and many souls who know the cross are failing to distinguish between the "will of God" and the "will of Satan"; and they are presenting *no resistance,* and no solid front against the adversary and his hosts. Surrender to God has lapsed into "passivity," or passive endurance of everything. They have only the view of the Lamb, and not the *Lion*-Lamb— of the Lamb who submits to death, but not the LION–LAMB who triumphs over the devil.

These souls must arise out of their passive condition, and in the power of the Spirit go forward into aggressive warfare against the powers of darkness. They must use their renewed will in *active* co-operation with God. They must take the offensive with victory-prayer against every hindrance that the devil puts in their way. They should march forward claiming the victory of the cross over all the power of the enemy. These are the souls who, because of their baptism into death and consequent cessation of fleshly and soulish energy, may receive or "take" and *exercise* the "gifts of the Spirit." Whatever gift is necessary for their service in this warfare they may *take it* as part of the provided equipment of the Spirit for this hour of need.

Note also that souls in each plane can help and lead others in the plane behind them, but they cannot push anyone forward into the plane before them, nor fully understand or "judge" others in the plane ahead of them. In the path ahead there are conditions and realms of knowledge and points of danger known only to those in that degree, and unseen and not understood by souls in earlier degrees. The enemy knows this, and oft-times pushes a "babe" in the second plane to resist truths *only understood further on.* Yet the truths suited to planes three and four *must be spoken for those who need them.*

Lastly, let it be distinctly stated that this description of these degrees in the spiritual life of the believer is given from the experiential or subjective angle, and not from the judicial or positional side of truth, wherein a "babe in Christ" may be said to be as "complete in Him" from the moment of conversion as at the end of life. A child grows from the baby stage, degree after degree, into manhood—and likewise the believer (Philippians 3:13–14).

CHAPTER 6

WHAT "DEATH" WITH CHRIST IS NOT!

1. *A misconception of "surrender."*

IT IS a misconception of the truth of "death with Christ" to interpret it as meaning a will-less passivity, lack of "feeling," or an absence of volition in the practical life of the believer. This *passive* state is necessary for the practice of Spiritism and many other evil supernatural cults, but the Holy Spirit energizes the human spirit into an *active* personality.

Andrew Murray writes that the Spirit of God, as the Spirit of the Divine Personality, comes into us to be the *life-principle of our personality*—the new divine life-principle of our new personality! The Spirit of Christ—His inmost Self—becomes my inmost self! "He that is joined unto the Lord is *one spirit* [with Him]" (1 Corinthians 6:17). So as we yield ourselves, spirit, soul and body, to

Him without reserve, we do not *lose* our personality but it is renewed and strengthened, and made more usable and active, by the incoming of the Spirit of Christ Himself. A true "self-effacement" does not mean a state of unconsciousness, it means that you become more acutely conscious, both of things around you and, above all, of Christ Himself.

The only way you could know that Paul was "crucified" was that there was an *entire absence of the "I" motive* in all his words and actions. Souls who believe that "death with Christ" means that they become unconscious of their words or actions, without feeling or sensibility, will find that Satan will give them "unconsciousness"—a lack of proper concern for themselves or for others. Christians who cease to think, reason, will, remember, love, act, listen, speak—believing that God is to perform all these things *in* them and *for* them—really become "non-existent" on these points, and open the door for the spurious workings of demons: e.g., if a Christian expects "love" to flow through him with no action on his own part, a spurious "love" will be given by evil spirits, which will eventually pass away, leaving the person hard and incapable of feeling. An inflexible hardness, and the inability to feel for the suffering of others, is an outcome of

What "Death" With Christ Is Not! / 85

Satan's *counterfeit* of "crucified with Christ." Or there may be an apathetic inability to come to decisions or to act, and such souls become a dead weight upon the rest of the church of God. How often suffering is caused to others, and the one who causes it is quite unconscious of having done so. This is a danger point, for when Christ dwells in you by His Spirit, He releases your sensibilities and quickens them so that you know in a moment if you have said a word of offense to another, and you run to put it right. If a man walks in the light he stumbles not. He becomes spiritually intelligent in all his relationships with man and with God. That is the victorious life, a life produced by Christ which will bring us down alongside of every human being in need.

This misconception of "self-effacement" is the enemy's counterfeit of *true self-surrender,* which yields up to God every faculty of the being, and which the Spirit of God needs for whole-hearted co-operation with Him in His purposes for the life of the believer. "The fruit of the Spirit is . . . self-control." There should be at the back of every action a deliberate volition, and full knowledge of what you are saying or doing, as well as the faith that that is what God bids you do or say.

2. "Death with Christ" not a STATE of sinlessness.

We need to be very careful in the language we use, that it is entirely in accordance with the Word of God. The word "eradication" is not in the Bible, and if by it is meant the complete and absolute destruction of the "old creation," so that the man is sinless, and cannot sin, then it is indeed contrary to the Word of God. Avoid unscriptural language.

Do not be afraid to go to Romans 6:6—"Our old man was crucified with Christ." As you believe that, the Spirit of God will apply the power of Christ's death to your life moment by moment and keep it a *fact* in your experience, so that there is *no foothold* for the enemy. That is, of course, assuming that you on your part will obey verse 11, "RECKON," and verse 12, "LET NOT sin reign in your mortal body." But do not fall into the mistake of thinking that you reach a *permanent position* where the enemy cannot re-enter, except as you walk in the light every moment, and in a very deep dependence upon the keeping power of God. It is necessary to walk very softly, and to be obedient to every bit of light God gives you.

If you think you have reached a permanent position, apart from this moment-by-moment faith, there is danger of not calling sin SIN. That is to say, there remains the danger of overlooking something that is unlike the Master and thinking it *cannot be "sin"* because the "old man" has been crucified. So the enemy can deceive you, and regain a footing without your knowing it. Any known sin must not be minimized or tolerated for a moment. IT MUST BE CAST OFF AND PUT AWAY, on the basis of Romans 6:6 and 12.... . On the *Godward* side, the cleansing power of the blood of Christ is needed continuously for those who seek to walk in the light, cleansing themselves from all defilement of flesh and spirit, perfecting holiness in the fear of God (2 Corinthians 7:1).

Keep to the Word of God, and do not be tossed about by every wind of doctrine; and take everything you hear to the Lord, and like a little child trust Him to teach you what *He* means by these things in His Own Word.

3. *A misconception of "suffering with Christ."*

There is a true suffering *with* Christ and a true suffering *for* Christ, but there is also the counterfeit of the enemy.

Last week a lady came to see me, at her wit's end over a case she had on hand. The light God gave me for her was that the pressure of her own spirit had grown so heavy that she could do nothing for that needy friend until she herself ceased to suffer for him. I said: "What good does your suffering do him? What good does it do anyone? None! It is sapping your strength, your power, your victory. It makes you spiritually feeble. You must refuse all needless suffering from the enemy. So long as he can drive the knife into you and you shiver, you will get the knife; but you can close yourself to it and refuse to accept it. Thus you will shut out of your life a great deal of suffering that will never do any good, either to yourself or others."

For many years I accepted suffering, and thought I was suffering for Christ. It did sometimes cross my mind how strange it was that I was always trying to get rid of this suffering, and yet I believed it was from God. If it was of God, why should I try to get rid of it? Then it dawned upon me that Satan can put suffering upon us. What God gives me I shall have His grace to bear, but I close my innermost being to unnecessary suffering produced by Satan. I remember a terrible attack of the enemy upon me, and I knew the enemy was saying to me, "Cry! Cry!" But I said, "I will not cry! I have no strength to spare, and if I do I shall be fit for nothing tomorrow. I refuse!" And that sense of acute anguish, like a vise that had seized the heart, instantly ceased. I know I am speaking to the hearts of some of you, and I shall thank God if other souls may get such a deliverance from suffering.

CHAPTER 7

THE APPROPRIATION OF TRUTH

TWO QUESTIONS ANSWERED

Q. Since Romans 6 declares that "our old man was crucified with Christ," ought we not to be thinking now about the resurrection side—"since ye then be risen with Christ"?

A. It is never safe to pick out one text and base your attitude upon that. You need the balance of truth. "Since ye then be risen with Christ"—yes, but remember that the reckoning yourself "dead indeed unto sin" is indissolubly linked with "alive unto God." Make the tree good and the fruit will be good, but if you try to put the fruit right first, you will go astray. God has blessed you "with all spiritual blessings in the heavenlies in Christ." Why have you not received them all? Because you have not appropriated them. He is waiting for you to acknowledge your need, to take your position "crucified" and "buried" with Christ, and then you will be in a position to "seek those things which are above, where Christ sitteth." The old-creation life produces nothing good, and God has sentenced it to death. The sentence has been carried out in your Substitute, and as you agree to that verdict and reckon upon that death as yours, the Holy Spirit makes it true and reveals the life of the Risen Lord in you.

It will bring confusion to imagine that you can reach a point of "death" once for all, and that afterwards you only look for resurrection life. In the experience of the believer, the two can only occur together—concurrently. Otherwise you must assume that you *now have* your resurrection body, and are sinless and incapable of going back from it. The truth is, you need to hold both a persistent attitude of "death" to the "old man," and a persistent counting upon the life of the New Man, which is the life of Christ in you.

I notice that believers are very anxious to jump to the resurrection side of the cross, but there is a danger of their thinking that the resurrection life is manifested in them when in reality a great deal of the old self-life is visible to others! We do not lack examples, unfortunately, of imitation "death" or imitation "life." If you truly desire the "life of Jesus" manifested in your mortal body (2 Corinthians 4:10), there must be a real working of His death in you also. So long as you are in your present body you are in a process of death and in a process of life—the one balancing the other.

On the other hand, you must not take the attitude that you are "going to die," but that you *"have died."* If you put it in the future tense, the full benefit of Christ's death is not wrought in you experientially. As the outward man perishes, so the inward man is renewed day by day (2 Corinthians 4:16). There is always a perishing of the outward, and always a renewing of the inward.

This persistent appropriating of the truth of Romans 6 destroys the power of the devil in your life and environment. *Your experience* does not destroy his power, but the death of Christ does. It would never do to rely upon our experience. We are delivered, not by *our* death but by Christ's death *applied to us* by the Holy Spirit. The finished work of Christ is not only that "He bore our sins in His own body on the tree," but also that "our old man" (i.e., that part of our being which causes us to sin) "was crucified with Him." How *much* of our "old man"? Ninety-nine parts? No, no! Christ's work was complete, and when He died, our "old man" was crucified in entirety. Therefore when you appropriate what is taught in Romans 6 you appropriate all the benefits of His death and the power of His risen life for that moment—FOR THAT MOMENT. And the next moment you appropriate it again, and then again. That is walking "in newness of life." It does not mean a constant struggle to hold this attitude, but as you rest upon the Word of God, believing that what He says of you in Romans 6 is true, you enter into the "rest of faith" concerning it, and the attitude becomes a habit of life.

Q. Is it wise to look into ourselves so much?

A. You must not look *into* yourself! You are *with* Christ, looking *at* yourself, and you do not look in order to be crushed by what you see, but so as to choose or refuse it. God will not change even the tone of your voice for you, as if you were a machine. He will put His laws into your mind and write them upon your heart, but you are the person to act upon them—and it is possible to have them in your mind and heart and *not* act upon them. It is for *you* to choose the way you will speak, think and act, and as you choose, the Holy Spirit will enable you to carry out God's laws. What we need is light upon our ways. If a man walk in the day he stumbleth not, because he can see.

May God give us light, so that we have no self-deception, and can bear the truth about ourselves, and know how to choose the good and to refuse the evil, by His grace.

Some books by the same writer—

THE CROSS OF CALVARY AND ITS MESSAGE
THY HIDDEN ONES
THE STORY OF JOB
THE SPIRITUAL WARFARE
SANCTUARY LIFE IN THE PSALMS
DYING TO LIVE
THE CONQUEST OF CANAAN

For particulars and prices of these
and other books, you should write to

Christian Literature Crusade
P.O. Box 1449
Fort Washington, PA 19034

Particulars of the magazine
The Overcomer may be obtained from:

The Overcomer Literature Trust
9-11 Clothier Road
Brislington, Bristol
Avon, BS4 5RL, England.